Rattle

By

Susan F. Carson

This story is for my grandson Ellis.

May his spirit always remain free.

At the beginning of a magical school year Paulita Romero walked into my life.

# Pauli and I taught a 4th grade class together.

Our students came from many walks of life. Most of them had one thing in common, they did not like school…yet!

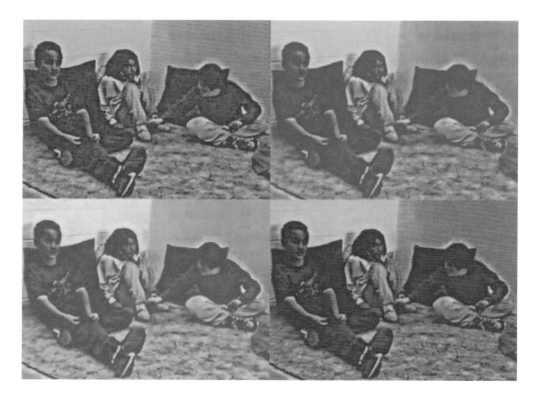

We all worked very hard that year.

Collectively we made our class into a family and our classroom into a very comfortable place to learn and grow.

We learned about one another.

Overtime we shared our strengths, challenges, likes and dislikes.

We learned as we explored reading, writing and arithmetic.

Our adventures included orienteering, engineering, puzzling, oceanography and applied mechanics
(very fancy words for inventing).

Sometimes our classroom became an ocean with whales drawn to scale circling above our heads.

At other times our classroom became a mountainous desert with sand baking under the hot sun.

Sometimes class was taught by Albert Einstein with the world shown in geometric shapes.

 Mavis Beacon taught us typing.

Bobby Fischer taught us chess.

We all taught one another and learned something very special-

about ourselves.

Pauli and her husband, John Romero, are members of the Tiwa-speaking Native American tribe of Pueblo people. Their home is the Taos Pueblo.

John experienced and was inspired by our hard work learning together.

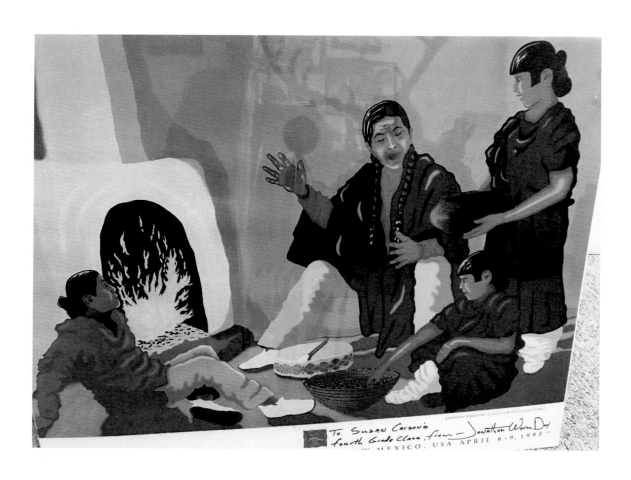

The Taos Pueblo, where Pauli and John lived, is the oldest home in all of the United States.

There have been many challenges to preserve the Pueblo culture.

Wars known as the Entradas between the Spanish colonists and the Pueblo people lasted over one hundred years.

Treaties were made and broken until the Pueblo people were left with nothing. Even Blue Lake sacred land was taken.

# Traditional dance and music

# were outlawed.

# Even traditional moccasins were taken away.

Children were sent to boarding schools such as the Santa Fe Indian School to erase the Pueblo culture.

Time passed and people learned about the mistakes made.

The Santa Fe Indian School now supports the culture and belief systems of children from 19 Pueblos of New Mexico.

# Blue Lake was returned to the Pueblo people.

# Now we all go to school together

and celebrate one another's heritage and culture.

At the end of our school year together,

John made me a very special gift.

A rattle. Chu, chu, chu.

Not just any rattle. One made by hand

just for me. This rattle represented

years of challenges and brought

traditions to life.

Ancient traditions were at work through John's practiced hands.

He told me that the carvings on the rattle

represented the many paths I would

travel.

This rattle has been with me from Taos, New Mexico to Eagle River, Alaska and Clarksville, Michigan.

It has been present at births, deaths and many adventures.

The morning after Christmas one year, my three-year-old grandson discovered the rattle in my meditation room.

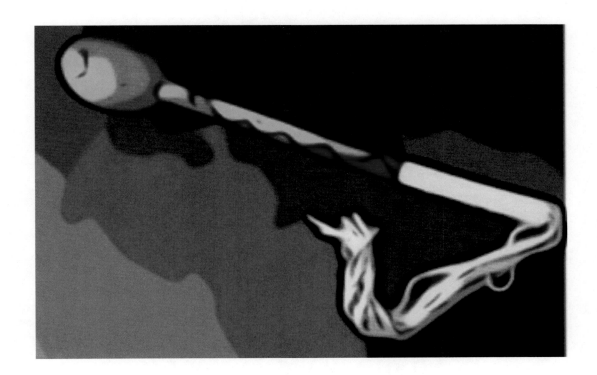

He threw it and it went sailing over the meditation room balcony.

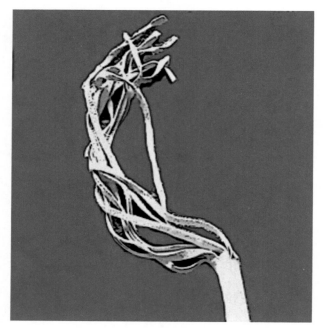

I felt it before I saw it. As I turned my head the white leather tassels swept through the air.

I jumped up and yelled,

"NO ELLIS!"

"NO ELLIS!"

"NO ELLIS!"

It was too late. The gourd resounded with a crack.

Healing happened. The rattle was carefully glued back together again.

Chu, chu, chu the rattle sounds once again. It is calling upon ancient traditions of healing, learning and the  beauty of nature.

# Chu, chu, chu echoing peace and

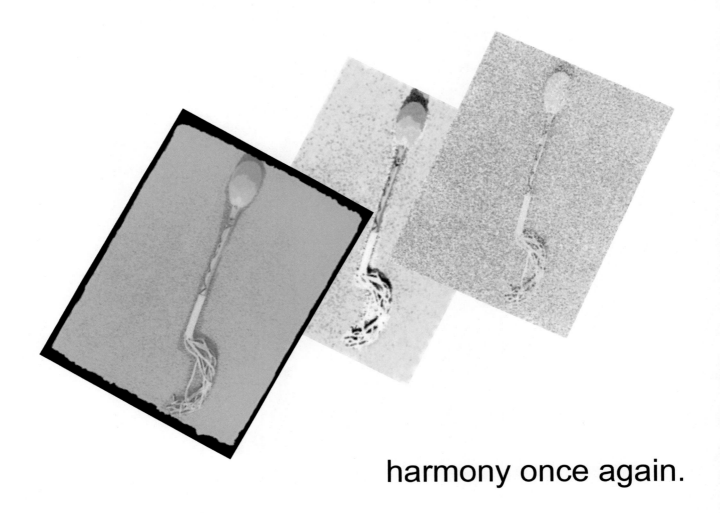

## harmony once again.

90406227R00027

Made in the USA
San Bernardino, CA
09 October 2018